25
Emergent Reader
Mini-Books
FAVORITE THEMES

by Maria Fleming

SCHOLASTIC
PROFESSIONAL BOOKS

New York • Toronto • London • Auckland • Sydney
Mexico City • New Delhi • Hong Kong • Buenos Aires

Cover design by Maria Lilja

Interior design by Sydney Wright

Cover and interior art by True Kelly except pages 5–14 by James Graham Hale

ISBN: 0-439-10435-1

Contents

How to Use This Book

Welcome to *25 Emergent Reader Mini-Books: Favorite Themes*! On the following pages, you'll find reproducible patterns for 25 mini-books that you can integrate into both your reading program and thematic studies on farms, weather, plants, the human body, and insects. Each book follows a simple story line on a topic that is familiar to children. By tapping into children's own prior knowledge and experiences, the books provide a natural way for students to connect with and remember language. And this in turn paves the way for successful and enjoyable reading experiences.

Some of the stories offer a silly or playful look at a topic, while others present a science or social studies concept in a more straightforward manner. All of the stories are designed to capture children's interest and imagination and build their confidence as readers.

The stories use rhyming and repetitive language and predictable language patterns to support emerging readers. You can use the books for shared and guided reading as well as paired and independent reading. The books also provide important at-home reading opportunities. Encourage students to share the mini-books with family members, both to develop their reading skills further and to foster pride by showing off those skills.

In addition to enhancing reading skills, the books can be used as springboards for a deeper exploration of a curricular theme or concept. On pages 5–14, you'll find suggestions for using the stories to launch theme-related projects and activities, plus reproducible charts, patterns, and manipulatives.

You'll also find that many of the mini-books work well as prompts for students' own writing. Children can innovate on the simple texts to create new books. For example, after reading "Farm Babies," students may enjoy writing a book about other kinds of animal babies by following the mini-book's language pattern. Similarly, children can use the mini-book "Sunny Days," which focuses on warm-weather outdoor activities, as a model for writing a book about rainy-day fun.

Whether it's to model writing, review a reading strategy, enhance a theme unit, stock a learning center, or nurture the home-school connection, we hope you'll find many uses for the 25 little books in this volume. And we hope your students will find 25 good reasons to keep reading.

Maria Fleming

How to Make the Mini-Books

Follow these steps to copy and put together the mini-books:

1 Remove the mini-book pages along the perforated lines. Make a double-sided copy on 8 ½- by 11-inch paper.

2 Cut the page in half along the solid line.

3 Place page 3 behind the title page.

4 Fold the pages in half along the dotted line. Check to be sure that the pages are in the proper order, and then staple them together along the book's spine.

NOTE: If you do not wish to make double-sided copies, you can photocopy single-sided copies of each page, cut apart the mini-book pages, and stack them together in order, with the title page on top. Staple the pages together along the left-hand side.

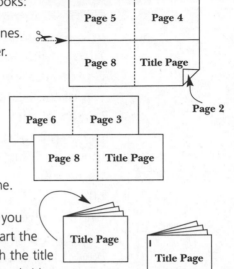

Activities Across the Curriculum

As you read through the stories, you're sure to think of dozens of ways they can be used as springboards to theme-related activities and projects. Here are a few ideas to get you started.

On the Farm

Farm Friends: Which farm animal is the class favorite? Let children each draw a picture of the farm animal they like best. Then use children's pictures to make a picture graph. Paste the pictures on a graph drawn onto a bulletin board or piece of oaktag. Use the graph for counting activities and to create simple computation problems (for example, "How many children like pigs better than goats?" and so on).

Food and More: Provide children with old magazines and ask them to cut out pictures of different products—such as milk, yogurt, ice cream, eggs, hamburger, bacon, wool clothing, and so on—that come from farm animals. Children can use the pictures to make a poster entitled "Gifts From the Farm."

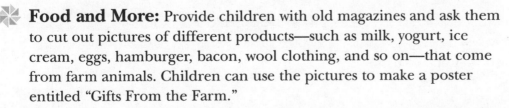

Wonderful Weather

What's the Weather?: Children can use the calendar grid on page 8 and weather symbols on page 9 to keep track of the weather during the course of a month. Distribute a copy of the grid to each child as well as a copy of the weather symbols. Discuss with students what type of weather each picture represents. Students can fill in the name of the month at the top of the grid, then fill in the dates in the upper right-hand corner of each box. (For younger children, you may want to fill in the numbers before photocopying the calendar.) Each day, invite students to paste a picture on the grid that best represents the weather for that day. At the end of the month, students can tally the total number of sunny days, rainy days, and so on, and use the information to answer comparative questions (for example, "How many more sunny days were there than rainy days this month?"). You may also want to use the calendar grid for other weather-tracking activities. During another month, students can record the temperature each day.

Plants and Seeds

Pretend You're a Seed: For a kinesthetic experience, have children act out the life cycle of a plant by developing movements to accompany each line of the chant below. Extend the lesson by writing each line of the rhyme on a sentence strip. Mix up the lines and place them in a pocket chart. Have volunteers put the sentences in the correct order.

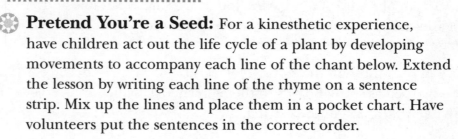

Fly, little seed! Whirl all around.

Fall, little seed! Fall to the ground.

Wait for a while, then it's time to SPROUT!

Now make lots of shiny green leaves pop out.

Grow taller and taller, take up more room.

Make a small bud, then bloom, bloom, bloom!

A Plate Full of Plants: Tell children that the plant foods we eat come from different parts of a plant. Provide each child with a copy of page 10. Have students cut apart the pictures of the different plant foods at the bottom of the page. Challenge them to figure out what part of the plant each food comes from and paste it onto the correct section of the plate. Extend the lesson by cutting out pictures of plant foods from magazines and inviting students to categorize them on a chart. (Answers: peas and corn are seeds; carrots and radishes are roots; celery and asparagus are stems; broccoli and cauliflower are flowers; spinach and lettuce are leaves; and tomatoes and cherries are fruits.)

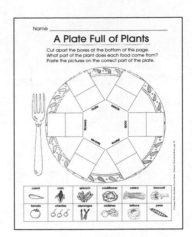

Me and My Body

 Mix and Match: On pages 11 and 12, you'll find cards that children can cut apart and use in a game of lotto to help reinforce the concept that different parts of our body perform different jobs—and what those jobs are. Divide the class into pairs or small groups, and provide each group with a set of the cards to play with. To make the lotto cards more durable and easier for kids to manipulate, you may want to photocopy them onto card stock. Students may enjoy making additional lotto cards for other parts of the body that they learn about.

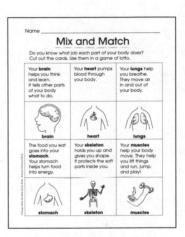

Bugs, Bugs, Bugs

 A Butterfly's Life: How does a caterpillar become a butterfly? Children can find out by assembling butterfly life cycle models using the patterns on pages 13 and 14. Provide each child with a copy of both pages. Have children begin by coloring the butterfly wings on page 13. (You may want to display pictures of different kinds of butterflies for inspiration, and point out the symmetrical design of their wing patterns.) Next, have children cut out the wings and glue them onto the butterfly's body on page 14. After the glue dries, direct students to fold the wings along the dashed lines to create flaps. Children can lift the butterfly wings in numerical order to learn more about the life cycle of these beautiful and fascinating insects.

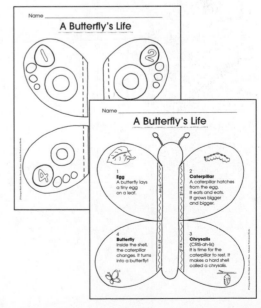

What's the Weather?

Use this calendar to keep track of the weather.

Sunday	Monday	Tuesday	Wednesday	Thursday	Friday	Saturday

25 Emergent Reader Mini-Books; Favorite Themes   Scholastic Professional Books

Name _____

What's the Weather?

Cut out the pictures. Paste a picture onto the calendar each day to show what the weather is like.

Name _____

A Plate Full of Plants

Cut apart the boxes at the bottom of this page.
What part of the plant does each food come from?
Paste the pictures on the correct part of the plate.

| carrot | corn | spinach | cauliflower | celery | broccoli |
| tomato | cherries | asparagus | radishes | lettuce | peas |

Mix and Match

Do you know what job each part of your body does?
Cut out the cards. Use them in a game of lotto.

Your **brain** helps you think and learn. It tells other parts of your body what to do.	Your **heart** pumps blood through your body.	Your **lungs** help you breathe. They move air in and out of your body.

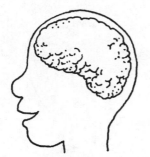

brain

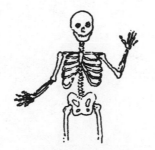

heart

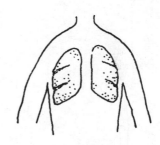

lungs

The food you eat goes into your **stomach**. Your stomach helps turn food into energy.	Your **skeleton** holds you up and gives you shape. It protects the soft parts inside you.	Your **muscles** help your body move. They help you lift things and run, jump, and play!

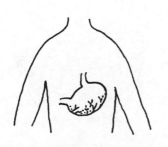

stomach

skeleton

muscles

25 Emergent Reader Mini-Books: Favorite Themes Scholastic Professional Books

Name _____

Mix and Match

Do you know what job each part of your body does?
Cut out the cards. Use them in a game of lotto.

Your **eyes** help you see.	Your **nose** helps you smell things. It also helps you breathe.	Your **ears** help you hear sounds.
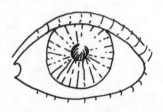 **eye**	 **nose**	 **ear**
Your **tongue** lets you taste things.	Your **skin** covers up all of your inside parts and protects them. It tells you how something feels when you touch it.	Your **teeth** tear and grind food into smaller pieces.
 **tongue**	 **skin**	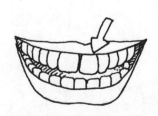 **teeth**

25 Emergent Reader Mini-Books: Favorite Themes Scholastic Professional Books

Name _____

A Butterfly's Life

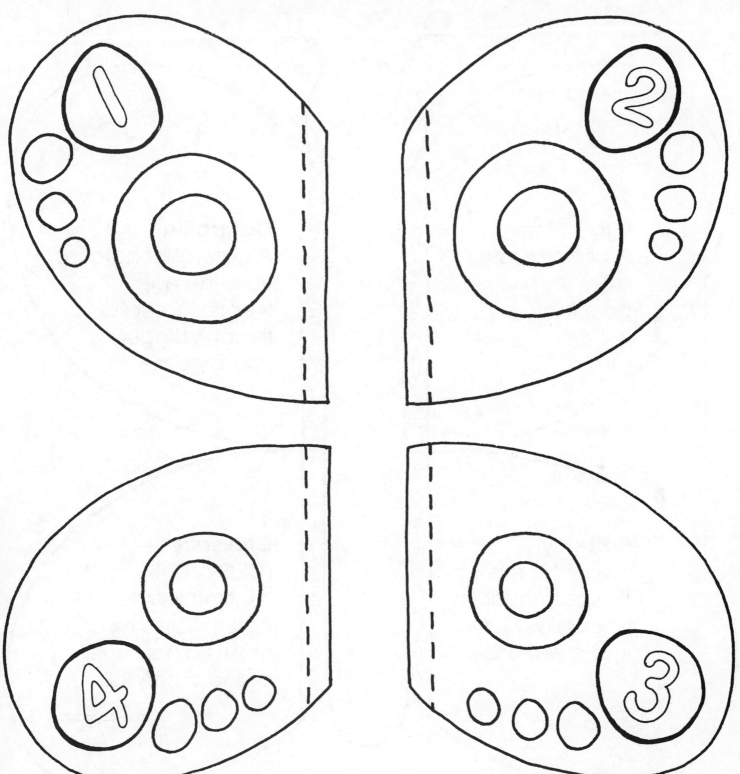

Name _____

A Butterfly's Life

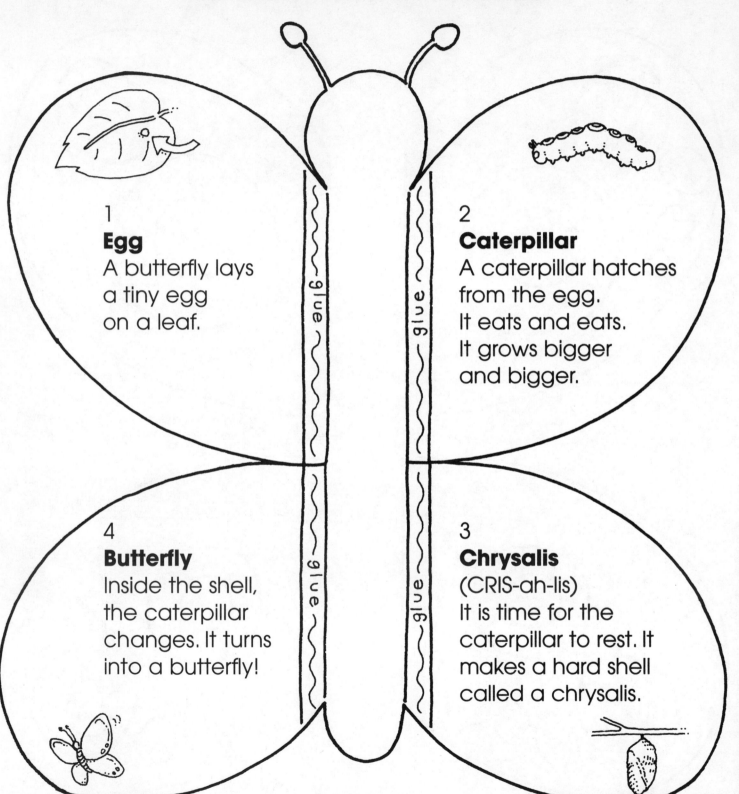

1
Egg
A butterfly lays
a tiny egg
on a leaf.

2
Caterpillar
A caterpillar hatches
from the egg.
It eats and eats.
It grows bigger
and bigger.

4
Butterfly
Inside the shell,
the caterpillar
changes. It turns
into a butterfly!

3
Chrysalis
(CRIS-ah-lis)
It is time for the
caterpillar to rest. It
makes a hard shell
called a chrysalis.

glue

Pigs on a bus.

Pigs All Around

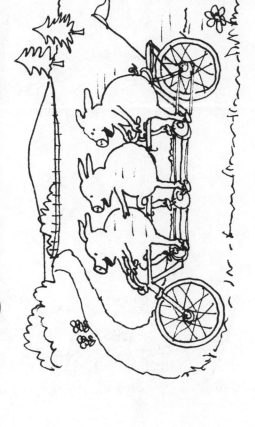

Pigs in a pool.

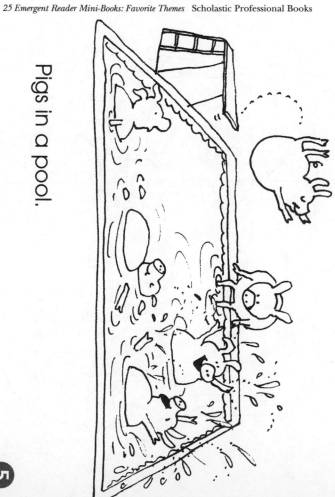

Pigs on a farm where pigs should be!

Pigs at a park.

Pigs at school.

Pigs in a tree.

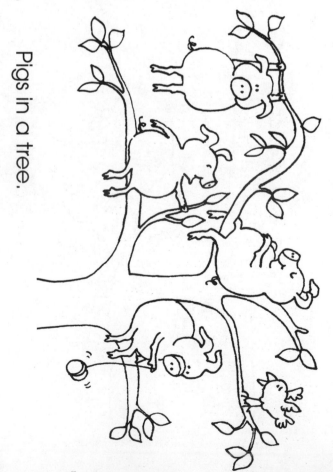

Pigs at a movie.

And that hen house had a hen.

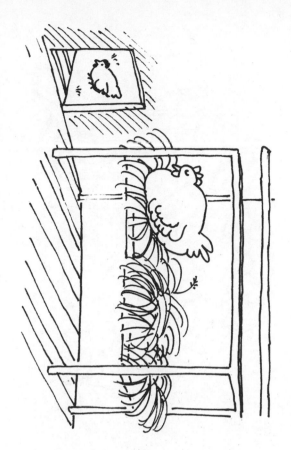

The Story of an Egg

And that hen had an egg.

I'm hungry!

There once was a farm.

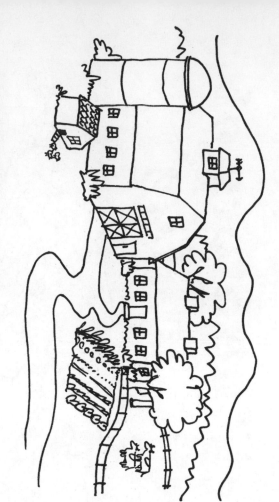

And that farm had a hen house.

25 Emergent Reader Mini-Books: Favorite Themes Scholastic Professional Books

And that chick had something to say.

And that egg had a chick.

If I were a duck I'd say, "Quack!"

Quack!

If I Were a Sheep

If I were a rooster I'd say,
"Cock-a-doodle-doo!"

Cock-a-doodle-doo!

If I were a farmer I'd say,
"Everyone be quiet!
I'm trying to get some sleep!"

Be quiet!

If I were a sheep I'd say, "Baaahhh!"

If I were a cow I'd say, "Moo!"

25 Emergent Reader Mini-Books: Favorite Themes Scholastic Professional Books

If I were a chick I'd say, "Cheep!"

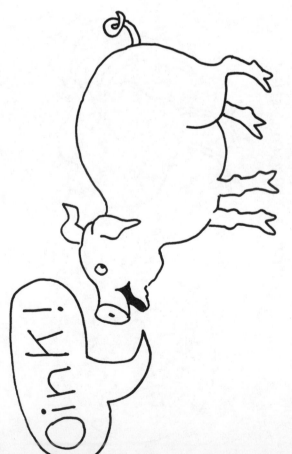

If I were a pig I'd say, "Oink!"

A baby duck is called a duckling.
Happy birthday, little duckling!

Farm Babies

A baby cow is called a calf.
Happy birthday, little calf!

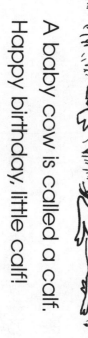

Happy birthday! Happy birthday!
Everybody sing
for all the baby farm animals
born in the spring!

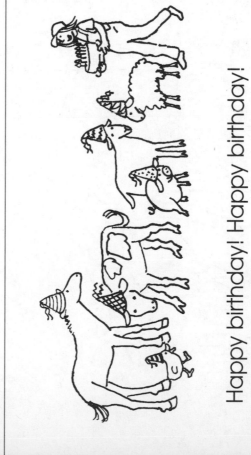

A baby pig is called a piglet.
Happy birthday, little piglet!

A baby sheep is called a lamb.
Happy birthday, little lamb!

A baby goat is called a kid.
Happy birthday, little kid!

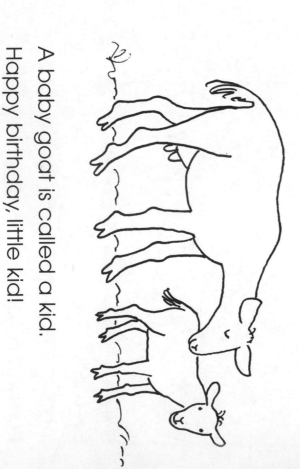

A baby horse is called a foal.
Happy birthday, little foal!

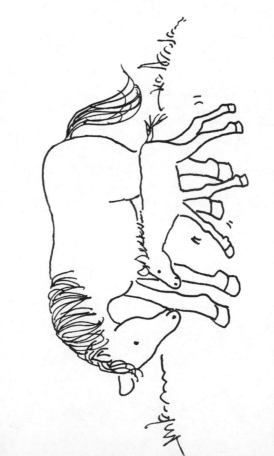

4

Follow me over.

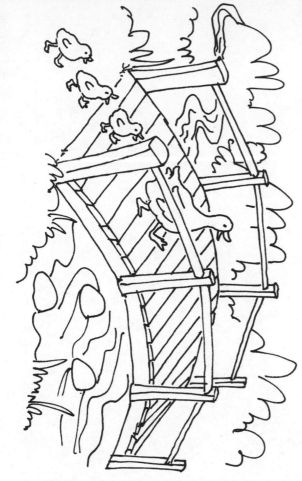

Follow Me

5

Follow me under.

Follow me home.

8

Follow me down.

Follow me up.

25 Emergent Reader Mini-Books: Favorite Themes Scholastic Professional Books

Follow me out.

Follow me in.

The rain rained on the mouse.

The rain rained on the frog.

I had my umbrella!

The rain rained on the cat.

The rain rained on the dog.

The rain rained on the bee.
But the rain didn't rain on me . . .

The rain rained on the rabbit.

Sunny days are hopscotch days.

Sunny Days

Sunny days are sand castle days.

Sunny days are the BEST days!

Sunny days are soccer days.

Sunny days are bicycle days.

Sunny days are ice cream days.

Sunny days are pool days.

Blow, wind, blow.
Blow the trees.

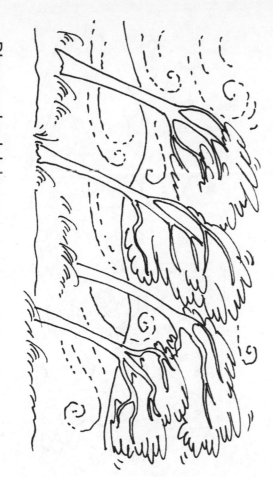

Blow, Wind, Blow

25 Emergent Reader Mini-Books: Favorite Themes   Scholastic Professional Books

Blow, wind, blow.
Blow the flags.

No, wind, no!
Don't blow me!

Blow, wind, blow.
Blow the leaves.

Blow, wind, blow.
Blow the papers.

Blow, wind, blow.
Blow the kites.

Blow, wind, blow.
Blow the hats.

Let's make a snow bear.

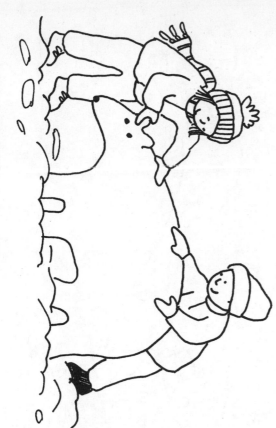

Snow Zoo

25 Emergent Reader Mini-Books: Favorite Themes Scholastic Professional Books

Let's make a snow snail.

And when we are done,
we will have a snow zoo!

Let's make a snow lion.

Let's make a snow whale.

Let's make a snow kangaroo.

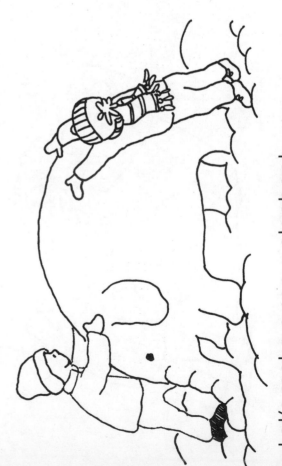

Let's make a snow elephant.

Sometimes it drizzles ...

What Will the Weather Be?

or rains a lot.

So remember to wear
the right kind of clothes!

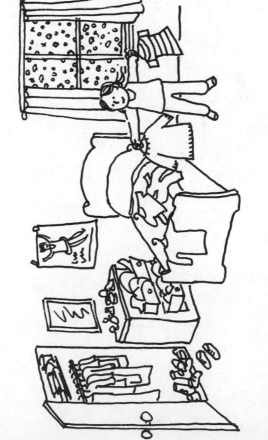

2

Sometimes it's cold.

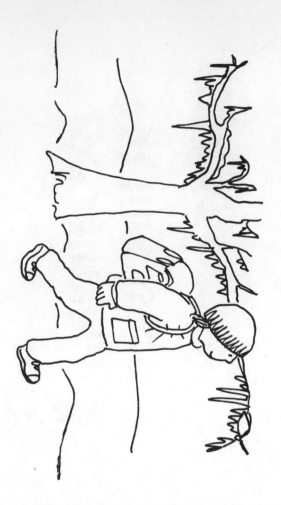

3

Sometimes it's hot.

25 Emergent Reader Mini-Books: Favorite Themes Scholastic Professional Books

Sometimes it snows.

7

Sometimes it's windy.

6

Will you be a tree?

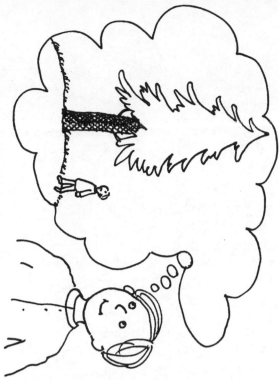

Will you be a blade of grass?

untill I plant you in the ground!

Will you be a flower?

Little seed, little seed,
what will you be?

Or a pumpkin, big and round?

I guess I will not know . . .

Just enough water.

What Does a Seed Need?

25 Emergent Reader Mini-Books: Favorite Themes Scholastic Professional Books

Just enough sun.

your seed will grow!

What does a seed need to grow?

Just enough dirt.

And before you know ...

Just enough time.

4

Watch my stem begin to sprout.
Watch my new green leaves pop out.

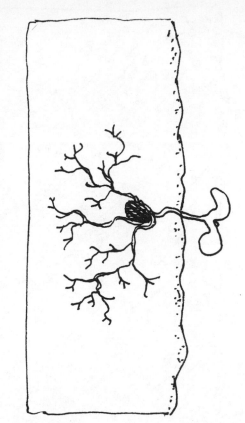

Watch me grow and grow and grow.

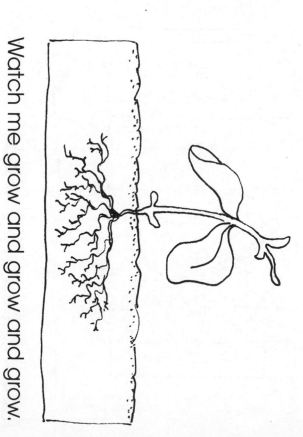

5

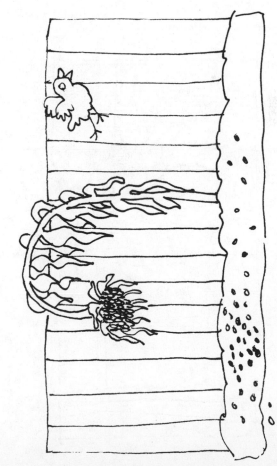

watch me make new seeds
to plant again!

8

I am a seed, small and round.

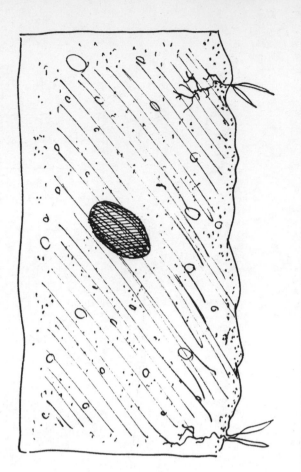

Watch my roots grow underground.

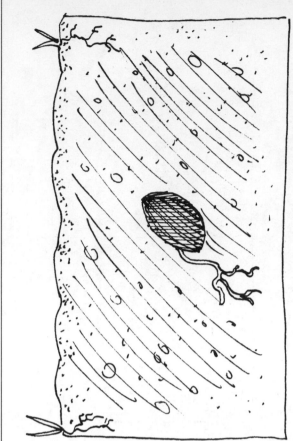

Watch my flower bloom and then . . .

Watch my bud begin to show.

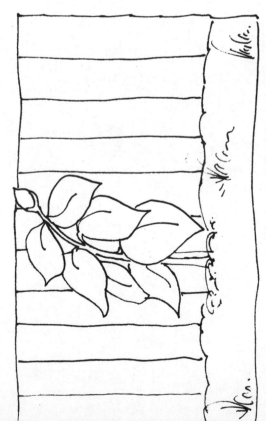

Row by row, row by row,
we'll plant peppers
and watch them grow.

Row by Row

Row by row, row by row,
we'll plant lettuce
and watch it grow.

and eat them, too!

Row by row, row by row,
we'll plant tomatoes
and watch them grow.

Row by row, row by row,
we'll plant peas
and watch them grow.

Me and you, me and you,
we'll pick the vegetables we grew . . .

Row by row, row by row,
we'll plant corn
and watch it grow.

What grows underground?
Potatoes grow underground.

What Grows Underground?

What grows underground?
Onions grow underground.

Dinner!

What grows underground?
Carrots grow underground.

What grows underground?
Radishes grow underground.

What grows underground?

What grows underground?
Peanuts grow underground.

Inside of me, there are lungs.

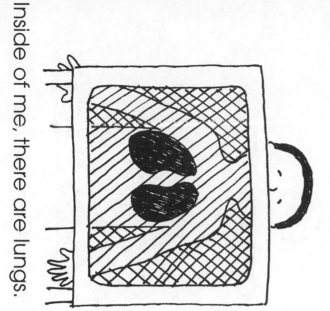

Inside of Me

Inside of me, there is a heart.

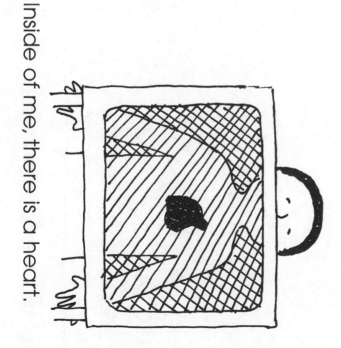

Inside of you, inside of you,
there are all of these parts, too.
And each one has a job to do!

Inside of me, inside of me,
there are parts you cannot see.

Inside of me, there are bones.

Inside of me, there is a brain.

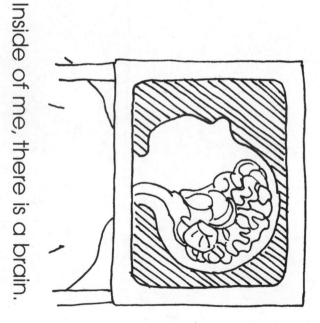

Inside of me, there is a stomach.

They can kick.

Feet Are Neat

They can slide.

Whoops!
And now and then, they even trip.

Feet are neat!
They can jump.

They can ride.

They can skip.

They can dance.

4

On Tuesday, I wiggled it. I jiggled it.
But my tooth would not fall out.

On Wednesday, I wiggled it. I jiggled it.
But my tooth would not fall out.

4

5

My tooth fell out!
Hooray!

8

On Monday, I wiggled it. I jiggled it.
But my tooth would not fall out.

My tooth is loose.
But it won't fall out.

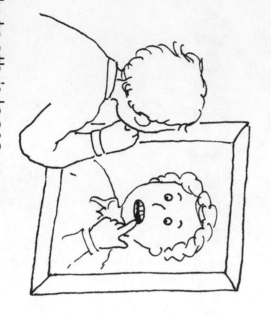

On Thursday, I wiggled it. I jiggled it.
But my tooth would not fall out.

On Friday, I did not wiggle it.
I did not jiggle it.
Can you guess what happened?

25 *Emergent Reader Mini-Books: Favorite Themes*   Scholastic Professional Books

I am smaller than my mother.

I Am Small

25 Emergent Reader Mini-Books: Favorite Themes Scholastic Professional Books

I am smaller than my sister.

I'll grow!

I am small.

I am smaller than my father.

I am the smallest in my family,
but that's okay because I know ...

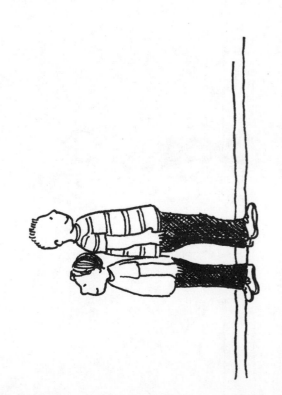

I am smaller than my brother.

I like my shape.

I like my size.

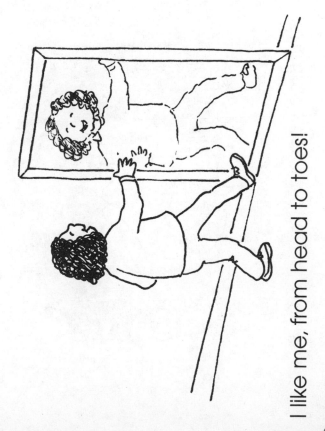

I like me, from head to toes!

I like my smile.

I like my eyes.

25 Emergent Reader Mini-Books: Favorite Themes   Scholastic Professional Books

I like my nose.

I like my hair.

I will measure a dog.

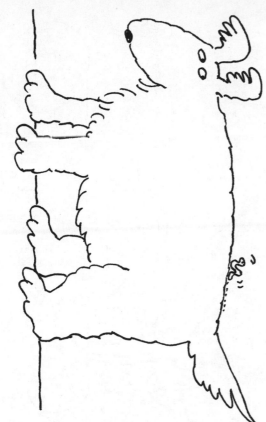

Inchworm, Inchworm

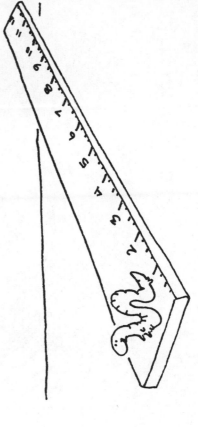

25 Emergent Reader Mini-Books: Favorite Themes   Scholastic Professional Books

I will measure a box.

I will even measure a dinosaur.
But it might take me a while!

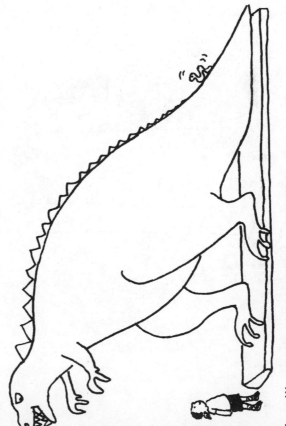

Inchworm, inchworm,
what will you measure?

I will measure a log.

25 Emergent Reader Mini-Books: Favorite Themes   Scholastic Professional Books

I will measure a door.

I will measure your socks.

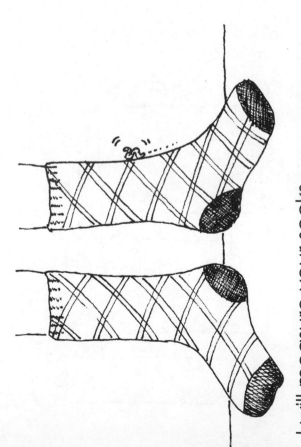

No, it is a shirt.

25 Emergent Reader Mini-Books: Favorite Themes   Scholastic Professional Books

Is this my flower?

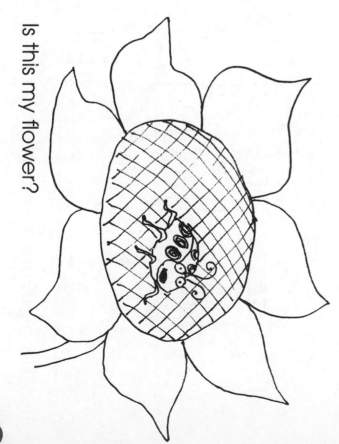

Is This My Flower?

Yes! Welcome home, ladybug!

Is this my flower?
No, it is a hat.

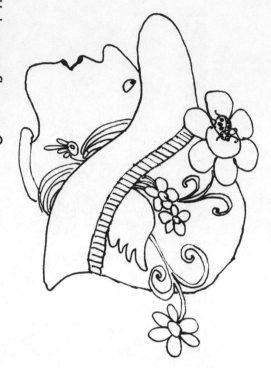

Is this my flower?

Is this my flower?

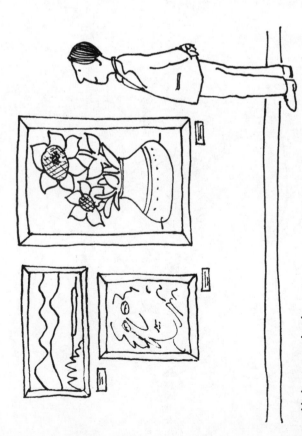

No, it is a picture.

Six by six, six by six,
the ants are marching up the bricks.

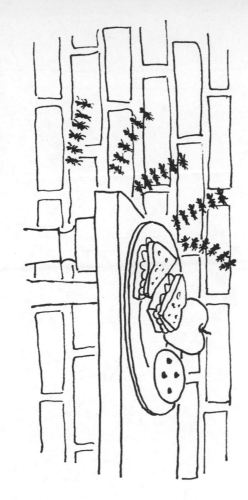

The Ants Are Marching

Eight by eight, eight by eight,
the ants are marching across the plate.

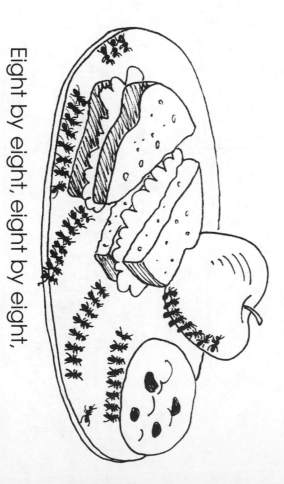

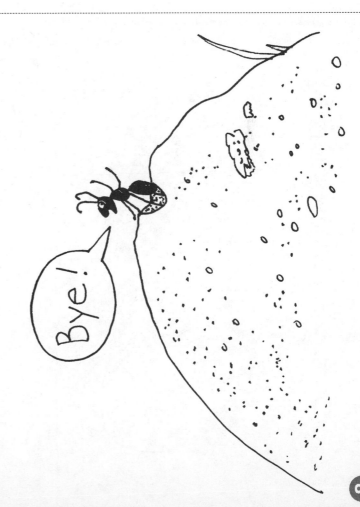

Bye!

Two by two, two by two,
the ants are marching across my shoe.

Four by four, four by four,
the ants are marching through the door.

the ants are marching home again.

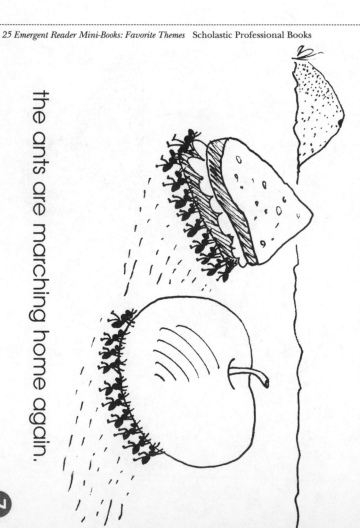

Ten by ten, ten by ten,

4

A kite can fly.
Why can't I?

Why Can't I Fly?

25 Emergent Reader Mini-Books: Favorite Themes Scholastic Professional Books

5

A bee can fly.
Why can't I?

8

Yippee!

. . . that you can
fly like me!

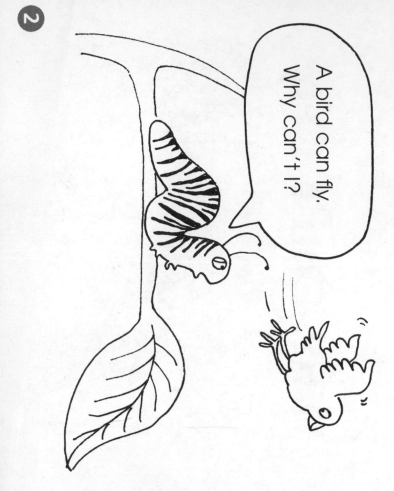

A bird can fly.
Why can't I?

A plane can fly.
Why can't I?

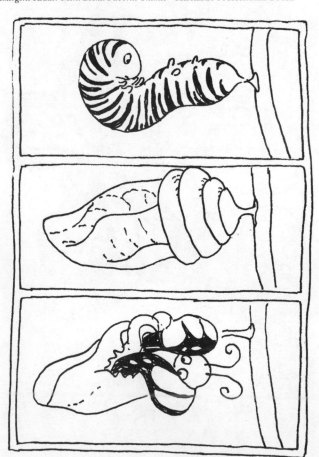

Wait a while,
then you'll see . . .

Flutter past the squirrels.

Flutter past the window.

Flutter, flutter, butterfly, flutter here to me.

Flutter, flutter, butterfly.

Flutter past the flowers.

Flutter past the rabbit.
Flutter past the tree.

Flutter past the boys and girls.